CHEESEMAKING: HOW TO MAKE BRIE AND CAMEMBERT

Simple and Gourmet Brie-and-Camembert-Inspired Recipes Paired with Wine

By Shari Darling
www.understandpublishing.com

Shari Darling is Canada's only aboriginal wine writer and has been a standing member of the Wine Writers' Circle of Canada for over 18 years. She is an International award winning and best selling author and columnist, educator, speaker, TV and radio host and wine judge who specializes in wine and food.

Shari is also the creator of many wine-learning tools, such as the 3 Secrets Wine Pairing Master Class and this series of cookbooks under the label, The Wine Pairing Club Presents.

Shari's work in sensory science as it pertains to wine and food pairing and her learning tools is utilized in colleges and universities throughout Canada for chef and sommelier training.

Shari has been a columnist for the Peterborough Examiner (Sun Media) in Peterborough, Ontario, for over a decade and writes for several other magazines.

In her hometown, she operates a cooking and wine club. Through the club she teaches cooking and cheese making classes, wine workshops, and wine pairing dinners.

The 3 Wine Secrets Master Class arms wine and food lovers with the tools they need to transform an ordinary dinner into a gourmet, culinary affair.

http://winesecrets.sharidarling.com

"The Wine Pairing Club Presents" cookbooks can be found by clicking the link below:

http://understandpublishing.com/visit/winepairingclub/

Join the Wine Pairing Club Facebook group at:

http://sharidarling.com/facebookwinepairingclub

For additional information please contact:
Understand Publishing **http://understandpublishing.com**
Shari Darling at shariLdarling@gmail.com

Special Thanks to my Editor,
Deanna Shanti, Shanti Publishing

To support you in your journey and to check out our other books in this genre and others go to **http://understandpublishing.com** and click the icon called "Our Books".

Table of Contents

Introduction:

I've been an avid cheese lover all of my adult life. In fact I wrote a book called 'Wine Pairing Club: The Wine and Cheese Lovers' Cookbook.' Writing this book gave me a mission or perhaps an excuse to develop and recipe test dishes celebrating a plethora of cheeses from around the world.

I also make cheese and have done so for several years. I re-discovered the art of making artisan cheese by instinct. In preparing a menu for entertaining, I decided to try my hand at making homemade mozzarella. I called a friend of mine, Cindy Hope, who is an award-winning maker of fresh goat cheese. I asked Cindy if I could buy fresh goat's milk and rennet from her. She generously provided both to me at no cost. So, in return I decided to purchase some of her handmade goat's milk soaps. Her soaps are magnificent.

That afternoon I made cheese — goat's milk mozzarella. Using the cheese I prepared hors d'oeuvres consisting of a thin slice of toasted bagel topped with fresh ricotta, a slice of green apple, a thin slice of my goat's milk mozzarella and drizzled the nuggets in honey. The sweetness in this hors d'oeuvre from the apple and honey demanded a wine to match. Italian Moscato was the wine of choice, offering enough sweetness to harmonize with the hors d'oeuvre. My guests were first excited to try my cheese and impressed by both the cheese, the hors d'oeuvre and it's pairing to wine.

That evening was the revival of my passion and mission to master the art of making cheeses at home and then using them in recipes to pair with wine.

Making cheese is similar to baking. When you're working with living cultures you're in a partnership with Mother Nature and Mother Nature will always win if you get sloppy. You've got to let her do her part, which is to ferment the cheese. If you use poor quality, old or ultra pasteurized milk or you fidget too much with the curds or you try to speed up the process by heating the milk too quickly you'll end up with a batch of soured milk rather than cheese.

It is such a simple process if you just follow the instructions. Winging it-- adding a little of this and that to the basic process or not measuring your acids and cultures -- will only produce poor results. Use the appropriate ingredients and follow the instructions.

I've also learned that one's home environment plays a role in whether certain milks will ferment and coagulate. I have a student who attempted to make cream cheese and failed several times. The reason is that she lives in a farmhouse with drafts. The interior of the house is cold. The environment was too cold for the milk to sour and coagulate. I suggested she put the batch in the oven under a lamp rather than on the counter. It worked.

The quality of the milk used and its level of pasteurization also play a major role in the taste, texture and quality of the cheese you intend to produce.

I've been making fresh cheeses for a long time. It took a while before I could muster the courage to attempt the creation of homemade baby Brie and Camembert. But once I did, I never looked back. They are so simple to make, once you try and have the right ingredients.

Giving a friend with a small box of homemade artisan Brie or Camembert that you made will win you far more praise than a humdrum bottle of wine.

My first homemade baby Brie gave me so much joy. I felt like a true cheesemaker! In my province in Canada we have a handful of farms producing whole milk. We have water buffalo milk, sheep's milk and goat's milk, along with the milk of cows. So I've been experimenting with the different types of milks, all of which produce lovely Brie and Camembert cheeses.

Now it's your turn to take this cheesemaking journey!

Let’s get started…

Chapter 1: Things You Need to Know

What Milk is Best for Cheesemaking?

Choosing milk for cheesemaking can be challenging. It's important to find milk that has not been ultra-pasteurized. Most milk available at supermarkets is ultra-pasteurized to extend the shelf life. So it is best do research to find out where you can purchase milk outside of large supermarkets, a product that is raw or 'just' pasteurized. Talk to local farmers and other local cheese makers and have fun!

Do not open the milk or cream container until you are ready to make the cheese. Freshness is imperative. Two gallons of milk or cream produces roughly 4 (4-inch) wheels of baby Brie or Camembert. Support small and local farms and dairies. Once you have a milk source you like for making cheese, stick with that one. Always buy the freshest milk available.

Let's define the different kinds of milk.

Raw Milk: Raw milk is best to be used for the making of aged cheeses, where the cheese undergoes a natural pasteurization period over 60 days. Raw milk is generally fresher, produces stronger and firmer curds, possesses more flavor and makes more cheese (curds to whey). If you plan on aging your Brie or Camembert for more than 60 days you can use raw milk. Raw Milk comes from a cow, goat, sheep, or water buffalo. It is full of natural bacteria and organisms. Nowadays, raw and whole milk is challenging to find, unless you have a close relationship with a local farmer.

Making fresh cheese from raw milk is risky, due to potential pathogens that are not destroyed. My advice is to stick with 'just pasteurized' milk.

Pasteurization: This is the process of heat-treating milk for the purpose of destroying bacteria, protozoa, molds, and yeasts. This process was named after its inventor, Louis Pasteur. Pasteur and Claude Bernard completed the first pasteurization test on April 20, 1862.

Pasteurization kills dangerous pathogens that can cause diseases like listeria, bacteria found in soil, water and some animals, including poultry and cattle. It can be present in raw milk and live in food processing plants and can contaminate a variety of processed meats. Unlike other germs, listeria has the ability to grow in cold temperatures. This means it can survive in the refrigerator. Listeria is a disease that affects primarily pregnant women, newborns, adults with weakened immune systems, and the elderly.

For 'just pasteurization', the milk is heat treated to up to 172 degrees Fahrenheit for 15 seconds or more. This destroys the undesirable bacteria.

While pasteurization serves an important purpose in killing unwanted pathogens, it also weakens the cheese curds, making for an inferior fresh cheese. For this reason it is best to infuse the milk (to be used for cheesemaking) with calcium chloride. This ingredient is described later.

Ultra-Pasteurization: This process is used to extend the shelf life of supermarket milk. This means the milk is heated up to 212 degrees Fahrenheit for at least 1 second. All natural organisms in the milk, including those that are beneficial, are killed through this treatment. It also gives milk an almost cooked taste.

Ultra-High Pasteurization: This process sterilizes the milk. The milk is treated to 280 degrees Fahrenheit, rendering it free of all good and bad bacteria. It also renders it highly unfavorable for cheesemaking!

Ultra and ultra-high pasteurized milk are not good for artisan cheesemaking, as the proteins and enzymes are destroyed. Even an infusion of calcium chloride does not provide enough help to firm the curds. When using these styles of milk in cheesemaking the results are hit and miss. So if you purchase milk at the supermarket be prepared for soft and floppy curds.

Homogenization: This process ensures that the cream (which historically was considered the most valued part of the milk) is distributed evenly throughout the milk producing a consistency of fat, texture and flavor.

Calcium Chloride: This is a salt of calcium and chlorine and is added to milk before the cheesemaking process to restore the natural balance between the calcium and the protein in casein. It helps to firm up the curds that might otherwise be destroyed through aggressive pasteurization.

Ingredients for Brie and Camembert

Mesophilic Starters: Mesophilic bacteria are divided into 2 groups. They are lactic acid starters and aroma producing bacteria. Many cultures, in the making of cheese, combine both. Different mesophilic cultures produce different types of cheeses. Some are fashioned for the producing of fresh cheeses, while others are used for the making of Brie and Camembert or Havarti and Gouda, to name but a few. Mesophilic bacteria grow at low temperatures and are used primarily in the making of North American style cheeses.

Pencillium Candidum (White Mold): This is a species of fungus in the family called Trichocomaceae. It is used to make Brie and Camembert and Cambozola cheeses and gives the cheese its white crust and distinctive taste.

Coagulants (Rennet): Rennet is used to coagulate milk during the cheesemaking process. Have you heard the term curds and whey? Rennet contains enzymes that separate the fat-soluble curds from the water-soluble whey. It also helps to coagulate the milk while it is not too acidic and therefore still sweet. Rennet comes in liquid, tablet or powdered form. Rennet liquid and tablets should be stored in the freezer. Keep rennet away from light and heat as this causes it to break down.

Animal rennet comes from the fourth stomach of a calf and contains the enzymes rennin (chymosin) and pepsin. Before modernization, farmers would use the stomach from a slaughtered calf or kid to make rennet. The stomach was cleaned and salted and hung to dry in a cool place. For cheesemaking a small chunk was broken off and chopped into small pieces. It was then soaked in cool, fresh water for several hours before using.

Nowadays, natural calf rennet is used, as well as vegetable rennet made from plants. Some plant species have coagulating properties, such as the extracted bark of the fig tree.

Chymosin is a higher quality vegetarian rennet made from the genes of calf cells. These cells produce Chymosin, which acts exactly like animal rennet.

Note: Rennet requires non-chlorinated water. Chlorination destroys rennet's action abilities.

Cheese Salt: Salt is important to the cheesemaking process. It draws moisture from the curds, thus helping to drain more whey. And most importantly, salt halts the fermentation, thus controlling the production of lactic acid. It inhibits the growth of lactic bacteria near the end of the cheesemaking process, acts as a preservative and adds flavor.

Salt can also be rubbed onto the cheese to form a rind, such as in the making of Brie and Camembert, or added with water to form a brine solution for soaking (Gouda and Havarti) or preserving (Feta). Be sure to use non-iodized salt. Kosher salt is ideal.

Sanitation: When teaching cheesemaking workshops, I stress the importance of sanitizing all pots, utensils and equipment before starting the process. It is vital. If an item can't be boiled, it should be soaked in a bleach solution of about 1 oz. per gallon of water and thoroughly rinsed.

Pots – I use 2 pots during the making of fresh cheese. One pot is made of thick stainless steel. I utilize this pot for heating milk at high temperatures, such as in the making of fresh ricotta. Because the pot is thick, the heat treatment doesn't scar the bottom of the pot. I have another pot that I love due to its shape, but it's made of thin steel. I use this for making cheeses where higher temperature is not a requirement, as in the making of Brie and Camembert.

Thermometer: A digital or dial thermometer is key. It doesn't matter as long as it is accurate. Make sure the thermometer has a long stem so you can immerse it into the lower parts of the milk during the heating process.

Cheesecloth: This product is used for lining colanders and molds and for straining the curds. Don't skimp on buying cheesecloth. Better quality cheesecloth can be washed and reused. Good quality cloth will also hold the curds and allow the draining of the whey. A poor quality cloth allows both the curds and the whey to drain.

Stainless ladle with holes: I found my ladle on Amazon.com for only $7.00. A good quality ladle is important for stirring your milk and draining out curds.

Stainless straight blade knife: Don't invest in buying a knife for cheesemaking. Just use one from your chef set. It is used for cutting the curds.

Colander: I have several colanders that I use for making cheese. Be sure to find one that is deep. It is used for draining curds from the whey.

Measuring spoons: You'll need to measure out powdered citric acid.

Measuring cup: You'll need a measuring cup for measuring the water used for dissolving of the rennet tablets before adding it to the milk.

Preparation Area: I'm a bit of a bacteria freak, so I clean my entire kitchen before making cheese. This is also because I have cats. In any case, make sure you have an entirely clean, dirt and dust free kitchen. Use a mixture of water and peroxide to sterilize counters and utensils.

Warming/Heating Milk and Curds: When it comes to cheesemaking, patience is key. If you rush or walk away from the pot, you'll burn the milk. I seem to keep learning this lesson. Control your temperatures by using a cheese thermometer. Heat the milk slowly and consistently. Stir gently.

Adding Cultures: Be sure to measure the culture and only use what the recipe calls for. Sprinkle the culture on top of the milk. Let the culture sit for a minute before gently stirring it into the milk. Be sure to keep your cultures in the freezer.

Adding Rennet: Rennet is not expensive and can go a long way. Don't add more than required as it will cause the resulting cheese to have a bit of a bitter after taste. A quarter of a tablet in a quarter cup of non-chlorinated water is all that is needed when making cheese from a gallon of milk. Dilute the rennet in non-chlorinated cool water. Stir in an 'up and down motion' and then around the pot in both directions. Don't stir for too long – some recipes call for 5 minutes, I think this is far too long.

Checking For A Clean Break: This is a process that you can use to make sure the milk has curdled. Dip your clean finger into the milk. If the milk breaks from your finger it's ready for the next step. If the curd is mushy and falls back into the pot in broken pieces, it has not set.

The Recipes:
The recipes in this book refer to a wheel of baby Brie or Camembert that is 4-inches in diameter and 1.25 inches in thickness. A 4-inch wheel weights approximately 8.5 oz. (1/2 lb.).

So if a recipe calls for 1 lb. of cheese, you'll need 2 (4-inch) wheels.

Chapter 2: Making Homemade Baby Brie and Camembert

Authentic French Brie and French Camembert are both raw milk cheeses made from the exact same recipe. This is really the only similarity between them. Both cheeses come from different regions in Northern France. Their histories are also different. Brie's origin dates back to 774 C.E. Camembert came later, developed in 1791. It is believed that a priest from Brie gave the cheese recipe to a Camembert, Normandy farmer named Marie Harel.

Classically Brie is made from unpasteurized cream, while Camembert is made with unpasteurized milk. Hence their fat content varies. Camembert uses a stronger starter culture, as well, making for a stronger-tasting cheese.

Their smell, tastes and textures are also distinct. This is because of 'affinage'. Affinage is the French word to describe cheese ripening. Brie is meant to be consumed young, while Camembert tastes better when aged for 6 to 8 weeks. The age also affects the appearance, taste and texture of the cheese. Brie, because it is consumed young, is often whitish inside and possesses a light, buttery scent and flavor, a salty aftertaste and a springy texture. Camembert, with affinage, tends to be a deeper yellow colour, is funkier smelling and tasting with earthy, mushroom-like and barnyard aromas and flavors and has a runny texture.

Brie and Camembert's characteristics begin with terroir. Terroir is the French term to describe Mother Nature's fingerprint on a particular region or even a farm. It includes the species of the cow, the grass that the animal crazes upon, the milk produced from these specific animals and the cheese made. In North America we call this the 'somewhereness' of a farm or region. Every species of animal produces different qualities in the milk. The minerals, vitamins and character of the grass on which the animal grazes also affects the character of the milk. The milk's character affects the aromas and flavors of the resulting cheese.

Brie is generally larger than Camembert in size. A wheel of Brie is from 9 to 17-inches in diameter. Camembert comes in a smaller 4.5-inch wheel. However, today baby Brie is also made into a 4.5-inch wheel. The recipes in this book call for either Camembert (4.5-inch) wheel or baby Brie (4.5-inch) wheel.

The French take their Brie and Camembert as seriously as they take their wines.
Legally, Brie and Camembert can only be produced in the regions of Brie and Camembert (Normandy), France. It is the terroir of these two regions that makes the cheeses so revered and distinct.

The French government officially certified only 2 cheeses to be sold under the names 'Brie de Meaux' and 'Brie de Melun.' Both were granted protection through the quality government's control system called Appellation d'Origine Controlee (AOC). Both cheeses obtained their AOC status in 1980. This is the same quality control system used in the making of French wine.

The variety name 'Camembert de Normandie' was granted its AOC status in 1983 and then again in 1992. AOC Camembert can only be made from raw milk derived from 'Vaches Normandes' cows. This is a species of cow bred in the Normandy region in North West France. They are believed to be direct descendants of cattle imported to France by Viking settlers.

Officially Brie and Camembert (Normandy) can only be made in these regions of France where their distinctive terroir creates their uniqueness, quality and character.

Stabilizers

Outside of France, in other parts of the world, including North America, cheese producers often use a dairy stabilizer to extend the shelf life of their Brie and Camembert-styled cheeses. A stabilizer is a gum system (a blend of gums and sometimes insoluble fibers.) Extending the shelf life means keeping the cheese from naturally ripening. In essence, the cheese remains young and does not acquire that runny texture and depth of character, that earthiness. The beauty of making homemade Brie or Camembert-styled cheeses is that you don't need stabilizers. You can allow your cheeses to ripen naturally, thus increasing their character.

Only the French Make Real Brie and Camembert: Baby Brie and Camembert-Styled Cheeses:

You will obviously not be making at home authentic Brie and Camembert, unless of course you are a farmer living in one of these regions! In this book you will discover the art of making Baby-Brie and Camembert 'styled' cheeses.

Homemade Baby Brie and Camembert

Typically the bloomy-rind cheeses you make at home are Baby Brie (from 18% cream) or Camembert from whole milk. I suggest you hunt around your region to find a farmer who might sell unpasteurized milk or at least non-homogenized milk. Refrain from using ultra pasteurized milk sold in large supermarkets. You'll end up with flabby and weak curds. If you can find unpasteurized milk, be sure to let the cheese age for at least 60 days. As stated earlier in this book, affinage (aging) allows the cheese to undergo a natural pasteurization.

In surfing the Internet you might also find companies selling classic large Brie moulds. The moulds used can be food-grade plastic or stainless steel. (You can also make your own moulds by drilling draining holes into both large and small yogurt containers.)

Storing and Serving Homemade Baby Brie and Camembert-Styled Cheeses:

When entertaining, if your baby Brie or Camembert-styled cheese is hard and bland, it may be under-ripened. In this case, leave it wrapped, at room temperature, for a couple of hours before eating. A hard texture or discoloration may also mean the cheese was improperly wrapped and has dried out.

It is best to wrap your cheese in waxed or parchment paper and then in plastic wrap. If the cheese smells of ammonia and mold begins to form, discard the cheese.

To freeze, cut the cheese into smaller portions. Wrap it in parchment paper, then plastic wrap, then foil and store it in a heavy-duty freezer bag. Once thawed the cheese will lose its wonderful texture, but will still be flavorful enough to be utilized in recipes like lasagna or soups.

Brie and Camembert can be eaten on their own, of course. If ripened for several months, their flavors become stronger. Prior to eating, remove the cheese from the refrigerator and allow it to warm to room temperature. Slice the cheese into bite-sized pieces, served with crusty bread or on flavored crackers.

Depending on its ripeness, Brie and Camembert are complemented by a plethora of wines. Young Brie is springy and fruity and complements crisp, dry white wines like Sauvignon Blanc, Pinot Gris and Pinot Grigio. A brut sparkling wine is also harmonious. Camembert that has ripened for some time possesses earthier flavor and partners well with more full-bodied reds, such as Cabernet Sauvignon, Malbec and Cabernet Franc.

This book is filled with simple and easy-to-make recipes as well as sophisticated ones celebrating homemade baby Brie and homemade Camembert.

You can use either cheese in all the recipes. The recipes are also paired with harmonizing wines. Many of these recipes derive from my best-selling wine pairing cookbooks and cheese and cooking classes.

If you love cheese, I know you'll love trying the recipes as much as I enjoyed developing and testing them and eating them with family and friends.

Supplies:
large stainless steel stock pot
long stem thermometer
soup ladle

stainless steel perforated ladle
long curd knife (12-inches)
4 Camembert hoops (molds)
4 sushi roll bamboo mats
cheese salt (kosher salt)
wire cooling rack (used for baking)
plastic tub with lid that fits cooling rack
waxed paper or cheese paper

a cold ripening environment (50 to 54) degrees (basement cellar or refrigerator)

Homemade Camembert (or Baby Brie) Recipe
Makes 4 wheels (8.81 oz./250 grams each)

Recipe:
½ tsp. Calcium Chloride in ¼-cup of non-chlorinated water

2 gallons of cream or whole milk (or a combination of whole milk and cream)
½ tsp. mesophilic culture* (starter)*
¼ tsp. Penicillim candidum*
½ tsp. liquid rennet or ½ tablet dissolved in ¼-cup non-chlorinated water
kosher salt (or non-iodized) as needed

*Calcium Chloriade, Mesophilic culture, Penicillim candidum and rennet and Brie moulds are available in cheese making shops or online. Try Amazon.com

Sterilize all equipment. In a large metal pot, pour in cream. Add calcium chloride and gently stir. Add the mesophilic culture and Penicillim candidum. Then gently stir the milk to combine all the cultures into the cream.

Pour rennet into ¼ cup of non-chlorinated water. Add rennet bath to the cream. Stir cream gently again about 20 times. Over low heat, heat the cream to 90F. Once it has reached 90F, turn off the stove. Cover the pot and let sit for 60 minutes.

Using your finger, look for a clean break in the cream by sliding your knife into the curd at an angle and lifting some onto the side of the blade. If the curd breaks cleanly around the knife and the whey runs into the crack in the cream, you have a clean break.

Using your long knife, cut the curds into a checkered pattern, into ½-inch cubes. Cut diagonally, as well. Stir the curds, breaking up the larger chunks. Let the curds sit for another 30 minutes to expel more whey. The curds mass will sink to the bottom of the pot. Using a soup ladle remove much of the watery whey.

Place 2 sushi mats in the kitchen sink. Place 4 hoops (molds) on top of the sushi mats (2 hoops per mat).

Using the perforated ladle, scoop the curds into the hoops. Fill the hoops just short of the top. Allow to drain so that you can add more curds to the molds. Keep filling until all the curds are in the hoops. Leave to drain for 1 hour. Place another sushi mat on top of the 2 hoops. Flip over the hoops. Repeat with the other 2 hoops. You are turning the cheese hoops upside down to drain. Do this every hour for 5 hours.

Let cheese drain for 24 hours. Remove the cheese from its hoops. The hoops slip off easily. Using your fingers, salt all surfaces of the cheese. Don't worry about using too much salt. Let the cheeses sit for 10 minutes.

Place a wire-cooling rack into plastic tub. (I purchased my cooling rack and plastic tub at Walmart.) Place parchment paper on the wire cooling rack. Sit the cheese on the parchment paper. The parchment keeps the cheese from sticking to the rack. The rack allows for aeration around the whole cheese. Cover the plastic tub with its lid. The plastic tub traps some of the moisture inside, creating a microclimate for the mold to grow on the cheese. Set the tub in a cool place at (50 to 54F) or in the refrigerator. (The cheese will take longer to develop the white mold in the refrigerator.)

After about 10 to 14 days the white mold will grow on the whole cheese. It may take a shorter or longer time, depending on your environmental temperature. (If any other molds grow on the cheese rub them off).

Flip the cheese daily. Also check for hard yellowing on the edges. This can be moisture that has dripped onto the cheese. Wipe away any moisture from inside of the tub.

Once the cheese is covered in white mold, it is ready to wrap. Wrap the cheese like a Christmas present with waxed paper. Place wrapped cheese back into the tub and let ripen for another 3 to 4 weeks.

Chapter 3: Hors D'oeuvres

Brie and Sage Pesto en Croute with Apples
Serves 4 to 6

Sage Pesto
¾-cup lightly packed fresh sage leaves (from 2 large bunches)
¾-cup pine nuts (about 4 ounces)
¼-cup (packed) fresh Italian parsley leaves
1 garlic clove
¾-cup plus 3 tbsp. extra virgin olive oil
6 tablespoons freshly grated Parmigiano-Reggiano
freshly ground black pepper to taste

1 loaf frozen bread dough or pizza dough, thawed
1 (4.5-inch/8 oz./227 g) homemade Brie or Camembert, rind removed*
½-cup sage pesto
egg wash (1 egg yolk beaten) with 1 tsp water
2 Granny Apples, thinly sliced (for garnish)
crackers (for garnish)

*To remove the rind use a cheese plan or vegetable peeler

To make pesto, using on/off turns of food processor or blender, blend sage leaves, pine nuts, parsley, and garlic until mixture is finely chopped. With machine running, add ¾- cup oil and blend until thick paste forms. Transfer to a bowl. Add Parmigiano. Season with pepper. (Can be made in advance and refrigerated until needed.)

Preheat oven to 375F. Divide dough in half. On a lightly floured work surface, roll each half into a 7-inch circle, just larger than the Brie. Place one circle on a greased baking sheet.

Cut cheese in half horizontally. Spread pesto over cheese. Place other half on top. Place cheese in center of dough on the baking sheet. Brush edge of dough with water. Wrap dough up around the cheese and seal seams together. The dough doesn't have to cover the cheese completely. Brush dough with egg yolk. Place a pan of hot water in bottom of oven to create steam, which keeps the crust tender. Bake bread for 25 to 30 minutes, until golden. Cool 5 minutes. Serve hot with crackers and slices of green apple.

Suggested Wine: The sweetness in the green apple requires a white wine with some sweetness, such as an off-dry Riesling or off-dry Gewurztraminer.

Camembert Pate

Serves 4 to 6

4 unpeeled cloves garlic
1 tbsp. finely chopped fresh rosemary
¼-cup olive oil
½ tsp. pink peppercorns
1 tbsp. hot water
2 (4.5-inch/8 oz./227 g) wheels of cold homemade Camembert or Brie, rind removed, cubed*

*To remove the rind use a cheese plan or vegetable peeler

Wrap garlic cloves tightly in aluminum foil. Roast at 300F for 1 hour. (I use my toaster oven.) Cool to room temperature. Peel cloves. In a blender or food processor, chop garlic, turning motor off and on. Add rosemary, olive oil, peppercorns and water. Blend for 30 seconds. Set aside. Place cheese in the top of a double broiler set over low heat; soften. In a bowl combine the cheese with rosemary/olive oil mixture. Whip with a fork until well blended. Transfer pate to a crock. Serve hot with Melba toasts or water crackers.

Suggested Wine: The earthy flavors of Camembert call out for a light, fruity red wine with some complexity, such as Pinot Noir or red Burgundy.

Ripened Camembert, Wild Mushroom and Rosemary Bruschetta
Serves 4

4 slices olive sourdough bread (1/2-inch thick)
2 cloves garlic
¼-cup olive oil
½ (4.5-inch/8 oz./227 g) wheel of homemade Brie or Camembert, thinly sliced
2 tbsp. butter
½-cup chopped shitake mushrooms
1 tbsp. fresh rosemary, finely chopped
kosher salt to taste
freshly ground black pepper to taste

Under broiler, grill one side of bread slices until golden, about 2 minutes. Rub toasted sides with garlic, and then drizzle with olive oil. In a saucepan, melt butter over low heat, then lightly sauté mushrooms, about 5 minutes. Stir in remaining ingredients. Top slices with mushroom mixture. Lay cheese slices on top of mushroom mixture. Under broiler, grill bruschetta slices until cheese begins to run. Serve immediately.

Suggested Wine: The earthiness of homemade Camembert and mushrooms and pleasant bitterness from fresh rosemary cry out for an austere red wine. Consider Cabernet Sauvignon, Malbec, and Pinotage.

Mini Potato Skins with Brie & Bacon

Serves 4-6
(Makes 24 mini potato skins)

12 small red potatoes, washed
corn oil (for deep-frying)
8 slices double-smoked bacon, diced
6 green onions, diced
3 cloves garlic, minced
12 sprigs fresh thyme, stems removed, leaves finely chopped
kosher salt to taste
freshly ground black pepper to taste
1 (4.5-inch/8 oz./227 g) wheel of homemade Brie or Camembert

Cut a thin slice off the top and bottom of each potato to make a flat surface for it to sit on. Cut the potato in half, parallel to the first 2 cuts. Using a melon baller or paring knife, scoop out the inside, leaving about 1/8-inch of potato with the skin. Put the potatoes into a large pot of cold water. Bring the water to a boil. Add salt. Cook the potatoes for 15 minutes, or until just before tender. Remove the potatoes from the pot using a slotted spoon. Transfer the potatoes to a cool water bath. Heat the oil to 375F in a large pot. Deep-fry the potato skins for 2 to 3 minutes, or until they're golden brown. Remove the skins using a slotted spoon. Drain on paper towel. Let them cool.

Preheat the oven to 375F. Sauté the bacon in a large skillet until it's almost cooked. Add the green onions, garlic and thyme to the skillet. Sauté the mixture for 2 minutes, or until it is aromatic. Season with salt and pepper. Chop the cheese into small cubes and place cubes in each hollowed-out skin. Place about 1 oz. of the onion mixture on top of the cheese. Place the potato skins on a rimmed baking sheet sprayed with nonstick cooking spray. Grill them for 10 minutes, or until the cheese is melted and the skins are hot. Serve hot or at room temperature.

Suggested Wine: The fattiness of the Brie and bacon requires a fatty white, such as barrel fermented and/or aged Chardonnay with at least 14% alcohol or an austere red wine like Malbec, Cabernet Sauvignon or Pinotage.

Pecan-Crusted Brie with Jalapeño
Serves 4 to 6

1 (4.5-inch/8 oz./227 g) wheel of homemade Brie or Camembert
1/3-cup walnuts
1/3-cup almonds
1/3-cup pecans
2 tbsp. sesame seeds
2 large eggs
peanut oil (for frying)
jalapeño jelly (of choice)
French-bread baguette, cut into 1/2-inch-thick slices

Freeze cheese for 30 minutes. In a food processor or blender grind all nuts and sesame seeds. Transfer nuts to medium bowl. In another medium bowl, whisk eggs to blend. Remove cheese from freezer. Dip cheese into egg mixture and then into nut mixture, turning to coat and pressing gently to adhere. Transfer coated cheese to a plate; cover with plastic and refrigerate until very cold, at least 45 minutes. (Can be made 6 hours ahead. Keep refrigerated.)

Pour enough peanut oil into heavy large skillet to reach depth of 1 ½-inches. Heat over medium-high heat to 350F. Fry cheese until deep golden brown, turning to fry other side. Using slotted spoon, transfer cheese to a plate with paper towels to drain. Serve the cheese with jalapeño jelly and baguette slices.

Suggested Wine: The heat and spice and sweetness of the jelly calls for an off-dry white wine to offset the heat and spice. Consider an off-dry Riesling or off-dry Gewurztraminer.

Chapter 4: Soups

French Onion Soup with Camembert and Rosemary
Serves 4 to 6

¼-cup unsalted butter
2 lb. medium onions, thinly sliced
3 sprigs fresh rosemary
2 bay leaves
3/4 tsp. kosher salt
2 tsp. all-purpose flour
¾-cup dry white wine
4-cups beef broth
1 ½-cups water
1/2 tsp. freshly ground black pepper
6 (1/2-inch-thick) diagonal slices of French baguette

1 (4.5-inch/8 oz./227 g) wheel of homemade Camembert or Brie, rind removed, sliced

In a large skillet, melt butter. Cook onions, rosemary, bay leaves, and salt over moderate heat, stirring constantly for about 45 minutes or until golden. Add flour and cook, stirring, 1 minute.

Stir in wine and cook, stirring, 2 minutes. Stir in broth, water, and pepper and simmer, uncovered, stirring occasionally, 30 minutes.

While soup simmers, put oven rack in middle position and preheat oven to 350F.
Put baguette slices on a large baking sheet and toast, turning over once, until completely golden, about 15 minutes. Add a slice of cheese to each slice.

Discard bay leaves and rosemary from the soup. Divide the soup between bowls. Add a slice of cheese to each soup. Place soup bowls filled with soup and with cheese on baking sheet. Place toasts with cheese on another baking sheet. Put both under the broiler. Broil 4 to 5 inches from heat until cheese is melted and bubbly, 1 to 2 minutes. Place a cheese toast in every soup and serve hot.

Suggested Wine: This soup typically tastes delicious when served with Pinot Noir.

Apple and Brie Soup
Serves 4

2 tbsp. butter
2 large apples (about 1 pound), peeled, cored, and cut into 1 inch cubes
1 sweet onion, peeled and roughly chopped
1 celery stalk, roughly chopped
2 tbsp. all-purpose flour
2 ½-cups chicken stock
freshly ground black pepper to taste
pinch ground cumin
pinch ground ginger

1 (4.5-inch/8 oz./227 g) homemade Brie or Camembert, rind cut off, cut into cubes
kosher salt to taste

¼-cup 18% cream (or half and half or fat free cream)

Melt the butter in a large pot over medium heat. Add the apples, onion and celery. Sauté until soft (about 8 - 10 minutes). Add the flour to make a roux (this is what will thicken the soup) and continue to cook for another 2 minutes.
Pour in the chicken stock while continuing to whisk the mixture. Add the pepper, cumin, and ginger. Bring to a boil. Reduce temperature to a simmer and continue to cook for 15 minutes.

Remove the mixture from heat and puree in a blender or food processor. Return the pureed mixture to the pot and bring back to a medium temperature. Add the cheese cubes. After the cheese has melted, mix together well. Add salt to your taste.
Just before serving whisk in the heavy cream. Serve hot.

Suggested Wine: The sweetness from the apples calls out for an off-dry Riesling or off-dry Gewurztraminer.

Wild Mushroom Soup with Sherry and Camembert
Serve 4 to 6

¼-cup butter
3 cups sliced large leeks (white parts only)
1-cup sliced, stemmed shiitake mushrooms
1-cup sliced crimini mushrooms, sliced
2 tbsp. all-purpose flour
4-cups chicken stock
1-cup whipping cream
2 tbsp. dry Sherry
4 green onions, sliced

12 1/4-inch-thick slices French-bread baguette

1 (4.5-inch/8 oz./227 g) wheel of homemade Brie or Camembert, frozen, rind removed, cut into 12 slices

2 tbsp. finely chopped fresh chives

In a large pot, melt butter over medium heat and add leeks and all mushrooms. Sauté for about 8 minutes. Add flour and stir for 1 more minute. Gradually mix in stock. Bring to boil, stirring frequently. Reduce the heat to low and simmer for another 10 minutes. Add whipping cream and Sherry. Simmer for another 5 minutes. Season to taste with salt and pepper. Fold in green onions.

Meanwhile preheat oven to 350F. Place bread slices on baking sheet. Bake until light golden, about 10 minutes. Cool. Top baguette slices with cheese slices.

Preheat broiler. Place baguette with cheese slices under broiler and broil until cheese has melted. Divide soup between bowls. Top each bowl with 2 cheese toasts. Sprinkle chives on cheese toasts and in soup. Serve hot.

Suggested Wine: The earthiness from the mushrooms in this soup require a wine with earthiness to match, such as a Pinot Noir or red Burgundy.

Stilton, Brie and Walnut Soup
Serves 4

2 tbsp. butter
1 onion, finely chopped
5 stalks celery, finely chopped
2 tbsp. all-purpose flour
2 ½-cups chicken stock
½-cup coarsely chopped walnuts
2/3-cup milk
1/4 lb. Stilton
1 (4.5-inch/8 oz./227 g) wheel of homemade Brie or Camembert
kosher salt to taste
freshly ground black pepper to taste

In a large saucepan over medium heat, melt butter; sauté onion and celery for 5 minutes or until tender. Stir in flour and cook another 2 minutes, stirring constantly. Stir in stock. Over high heat bring soup to a boil, stirring constantly until thickened. Lower heat and simmer, stirring occasionally, for 30 minutes. Transfer soup in batches to a blender or food processor. Add walnuts. Puree until smooth. Transfer soup to a clean saucepan. Stir in milk and heat over low heat. Slowly stir in Stilton and Brie, stirring constantly until well blended. Season soup with salt and pepper. Serve in heated bowls.

Suggested Wine: Choose an austere red with enough tannin and astringency (bitterness and tannin) to harmonize with the bitterness of walnuts, yet nicely offsetting the saltiness in Stilton. Consider Cabernet Sauvignon, Malbec, and Pinotage.

Lobster and Scallop Bisque with Camembert
Serves 4

1 (3 lb.) lobster
1 oz. sliced bacon (about 2 slices), chopped
2 large leeks (white and pale green parts only), washed, finely chopped (1 ½-cups)
1 tbsp. unsalted butter
1 large russet (baking) potato (3/4 lb.), diced
2 tbsp. dry white wine
1 (6-inch) fresh thyme sprig

1/4 tsp. white pepper
3 ½-cups bottled clam juice (28 ounces)
2 tbsp. butter.
1 large celery rib, cut into 1/3-inch dice (1/2 cup)
3/4 lb. sea scallops, tough muscle removed from side of each if required
½-cup whole milk
½ (4.5-inch/8 oz./227 g) wheel of homemade Camembert or Brie, rind removed
1/4 tsp. salt, or to taste

To cook lobster, fill a 6-quart kettle 3/4-full with salted water and bring to a boil. Plunge the tip of a sharp knife straight down right behind the lobster's eyes. Plunge lobster into water and cook, covered, over high heat for 8 minutes. Transfer lobster with tongs to a large bowl and in a measuring cup reserve 2 cups cooking liquid. Let lobster stand until cool enough to handle. Working over a bowl to catch the juices, twist off tail and claws and reserve juices. Reserve tomalley (soft green paste in body cavity) and discard head sacs and any roe. Remove meat from claws and tail, reserving shells and lobster body. (Lobster meat will not be cooked through.) Coarsely chop meat and transfer to a bowl. Chill lobster meat, covered, until needed.

Cook bacon in a skillet over moderate heat, stirring occasionally, until crisp, about 3 minutes, and transfer to paper towels to drain. Crumble bacon.

In a cast iron skillet melt butter over low heat. Cook half of leeks, covered, stirring occasionally, until very soft, about 10 minutes. Add to the cast iron skillet wine, thyme sprig, and white pepper. Bring to a boil until most of liquid is evaporated, about 1 minute. Add 1/3-cup of the potato (reserve remaining diced potato in a bowl of cold water), and clam juice. Simmer, uncovered, until potato is tender, about 15 minutes.

Remove and discard thyme sprig and purée soup in 2 batches in a blender until very smooth. Set aside. Clean saucepan.

Drain remaining potatoes in a colander. In the saucepan melt butter and sauté the potatoes and celery until just tender, about 5 minutes, then drain. Add soup from blender to saucepan. Add scallops, lobster meat, milk, cheese and salt and cook over moderate heat (do not let boil), stirring constantly for the cheese to melt and until scallops are just cooked through, about 2 minutes. Add more milk if bisque is too thick. Garnish with fresh herbs.

Suggested Wine: This dish is very rich and fatty, thus deserving of a big, fat white wine, such as barrel fermented and/or aged Chardonnay with at least 14% alcohol.

Soup of Mussels and Camembert
Serves 4

4 tsp. whey butter
1/3-cup diced leeks
2-cups fish stock
2/3-cups whipping cream
1 tsp. finely chopped shallots
1 clove garlic
4 tsp. vermouth
4 tsp. white wine
12 mussels, scrubbed and debearded
1 (4.5-inch/8 oz./227 g) wheel of homemade Camembert or Brie, diced
1 tbsp. crumbled Stilton
kosher salt and freshly ground black pepper to taste
4 sprigs fresh chervil

In a large saucepan over medium heat, melt butter; sauté leeks until soft. Add fish stock and simmer gently for 15 minutes. Set leeks on a plate. Bring fish stock to a simmer. Gradually stir in cream. Remove from heat.

In another saucepan over medium high heat, combine shallots, garlic, vermouth and wine; bring to a boil. Add mussels. Cover and steam for 3 to 5 minutes or until mussels have opened. Remove mussels with a slotted spoon. Discard unopened mussels. Shell mussels and keep warm. Stir mussel stock into the creamy stock and bring to a boil. Whisk in Camembert and Stilton. Season with salt and pepper. Place three mussels in the bottom of each heated bowl. Divide leeks evenly among bowls. Pour soup over mussels and leeks. Garnish each bowl with a chervil sprig.

Suggested Wine: Choose a big, fat white with enough fattiness to match the fattiness of butter, whipping cream, Brie and Stilton, such as a barrel fermented and/or aged Chardonnay with at least 14% alcohol.

Chapter 5: Salads and Savories

Pan-Fried Camembert with Redcurrant Sauce
Serves 4

2 (4.5-inch/8 oz./227 g) homemade Camembert or Brie, cut into 6 wedges
2/3-cup all-purpose flour
4 eggs, lightly whisked
2-cup dried breadcrumbs
1 jar redcurrant jelly
juice from lemon
1 tbsp. dry red wine
2 tsp. mustard
corn oil (for frying)
fresh greens (for garnish)

Freeze cheese wheels for at least 1 hour. In 3 separate bowls place flour, eggs and breadcrumbs. Toss the cheese wedge in flour.

Shake off excess flour. Dip into eggs and then dredge in breadcrumbs. Set on a plate lined with parchment paper. Repeat until all 12 wedges are done. Cover and refrigerate for at least 2 hours.

Meanwhile make redcurrant sauce. In a saucepan combine jelly, lemon juice, wine and mustard. Bring to a boil. Lower heat. Simmer until mixture thickens.

In a deep frying pan add corn oil, enough to cover wedges completely. Heat on medium high. To test when oil is ready, add a cube of bread. When it turns golden within 15 seconds, the oil is hot enough for the cheese. Add 3 to 4 wedges of cheeses at a time. When golden remove from heat and drain on paper towel. Fry all 12 wedges. Serve wedges on a platter with a bowl of sauce.

Suggested Wine: The sweetness in the sauce demands an off-dry Rose with enough sweetness to match the sweetness in the sauce, garnished with fresh greens.

Chicken Salad with Brie and Toasted Pecans
Serves 4

4 cups mixed greens
1 Anjou pear, sliced
½ (4.5-inch/8 oz./227 g) wheel of homemade Brie or Camembert, cubed
1/3 cup toasted pecans, chopped

Dressing:
2 tbsp white balsamic vinegar
1 tsp Dijon mustard
2 garlic clove, minced (optional)
1/4 tsp granulated sugar
kosher salt to taste
freshly ground black pepper
2 tbsp. extra virgin olive oil
2 tbsp. finely chopped fresh chives
1 tbsp. apple juice concentrate

12 ribbons (1/2-inch wide) of cooked chicken

In salad bowl combine lettuce pear, Brie and pecans.

Whisk together the vinegar, mustard, garlic, sugar, salt and pepper. In a steady stream pour in oil, whisking vigorously. Fold in chives. Mix in apple juice. Toss salad with dressing. Top with room temperature chicken ribbons. Serve.

Suggested Wine: The acidity in this dressing calls for a white wine with equal acidity, such as a crisp, dry white. Consider Sauvignon Blanc, Pinot Gris or Pinot Grigio.

Baby Asparagus, Camembert and Blueberry Salad
Serves 4 to 6

Blueberry Vinaigrette:
¼-cup extra virgin olive oil
1/3-cup white balsamic vinegar
¼-cup fresh blueberries

Salad:
3 bundles pencil-thin asparagus
1 (4.5-inch/8 oz./227 g) wheel of homemade Camembert or Brie, cubed
1 red onion, cut into thin rings
1 tbsp. finely chopped fresh basil
1 tbsp. finely chopped fresh parsley

To make vinaigrette, in a jar combine all vinaigrette ingredients. Shake well. Refrigerate for 1 hour. Plunge asparagus into boiling salted water. Cook briefly until bright green and tender-crisp. Drain and immediately rinse under cold water to preserve color and crispness. Toss asparagus with cheese, onion rings, basil and parsley. Shake vinaigrette well and pour desired amount over salad. Refrigerate remaining vinaigrette.

Suggested Wine: The acidity in the vinaigrette requires a white wine with more acidity, such as a brut sparkling wine or crisp, dry white wine. Consider Sauvignon Blanc, Pinot Gris or Pinot Grigio.

Brie Brioches on Greens with Raspberries
Serves 4 to 6

Salad:
1 head baby romaine lettuce
1 head oak-leaf lettuce
1 head radicchio
1 bunch watercress
2 tbsp. finely chopped fresh parsley

Vinaigrette:
1 tbsp. diced shallots
¼-cup white wine
¼-cup white balsamic vinegar
2/3-cup whipping cream
1/3-cup cold butter, diced

Brie Brioches:
1-cup milk
¼ lb. sweet butter
2 tbsp. granulated sugar
1 pkg. active dry yeast
2 tsp. kosher salt
2 small beaten eggs, room temperature
4-cups all-purpose flour, sifted
1 tbsp. vegetable oil
1 (4.5-inch/8 oz./227 g) wheel of homemade Brie or Camembert*
egg wash (1 egg beaten with 1 tsp. water)
fresh raspberries (for garnish)

*Use a cheese plane or vegetable peeler to remove the rind of the cheese.

Tear romaine, oak-leaf lettuce, radicchio and watercress into bite-sized pieces. Toss with parsley. Refrigerate until needed.

To make vinaigrette, in a small saucepan over medium heat combine shallots, white wine and vinegar. Simmer, stirring occasionally, until reduced and syrupy. In another small saucepan over medium heat, reduce cream, stirring constantly, until syrupy. Bring vinegar mixture to a boil. Add reduced cream, a little at a time, stirring constantly until well incorporated. Add diced butter, stirring until well blended. Set aside.

To make the brioches, in a saucepan combine milk, butter and sugar and bring to a boil. Remove pan from heat. Pour liquid into a bowl. Let cool to luke warm. Stir in yeast. Let stand for 10 minutes. Stir in salt and beaten eggs. Slowly add four, 1 cup at a time. Knead dough for 10 minutes and form into a ball. Coat the ball with oil. Set in a clean bowl. Cover bowl with plastic wrap and let rise to triple its size, about 2 hours.

Transfer dough to a lightly floured work surface and knead for 2 minutes. Return dough ball back to bowl, cover with towel and let rise to double its size, about 1 hour. Transfer dough to a lightly floured work surface. Divide the dough into 12 pieces. Flatten each piece into a circle. Place a cube of cheese in the centre of each circle. Pull up the dough around the cheese, completely enclosing it. Shape the dough into a ball and set into lightly greased muffin tins. Brush with egg-wash. Bake at 375F for 30 minutes or until golden. On chilled plates, arrange salad greens. Garnish with fresh raspberries. Set 2 brioches on each plate. Open brioches and drizzle centres with vinaigrette.

Suggested Wine: The red color of the vinaigrette and sweetness from the berries requires a wine with some sweetness to match. Consider an off-dry rose or white zinfandel with sweetness.

Mixed Salad of Greens with Honey Mustard Vinaigrette and Goat's Brie Toasts
Serves 4

½-cup walnuts (coarsely chopped)
2 tbsps. honey
1 1/2 tbsp. Dijon mustard
3 tbsp. white balsamic vinegar
1 1/2 tbsp. shallots (minced)
1/2 tsp. kosher salt
1/4 tsp. freshly ground black pepper
6 tbsp. vegetable oil

4 (1/2-inch) slices of French baguette
vegetable oil (as needed)
1 (4.5-inch/8 oz./227 g) homemade goat's milk Brie or Camembert *

10 oz. mixed greens (frisée, radicchio and mesclun)
½-cup toasted walnuts*

*Walnuts can be toasted in a dry fry pan.

To make the vinaigrette, combine the honey, Dijon mustard, vinegar, oil, shallots, salt and pepper in a sanitized glass jar. Cover and shake to emulsify. Set in refrigerator until needed.

In a cast iron skillet add ¼-inch of oil. Turn on high and when almost smoking, lay baguette slices in skillet. Fry for 30 seconds or until golden. Flip and fry the other side until golden. Drain on paper towel.

Preheat boiler. Slice 4 (1/4-inch) slices of cheese. Place slices on baguette slices. Place on baking sheet and broil until cheese has melted.

While baguette is under broiler, toss salad with vinaigrette as desired and sprinkle with walnuts. Place a Brie toast on each salad and serve.

Camembert and Wild Mushroom Quiche
Serves 4 to 6

1 tbsp. unsalted butter
1 clove garlic, minced
½-cup coarsely chopped fresh shiitake mushrooms

½ (4.5-inch/8 oz./227 g) wheel of homemade Camembert or Brie, room temperature, rind removed, diced*

1/3 lb. homemade cream cheese
4 eggs
kosher salt to taste
freshly ground black pepper to taste
pinch cayenne
1 tbsp. finely chopped fresh basil
1 unbaked (8-inch) single pie shell

*Use a cheese plane or vegetable peeler to remove rind of cheese. This recipe calls for a very ripened homemade Camembert (soft and creamy.)

In a small saucepan over medium heat, melt butter. Sauté garlic and mushrooms until tender. Set aside. In a large bowl combine the cheese with cream cheese. Using a fork, cream cheeses until all lumps are gone. Beat in eggs until mixture is smooth. Add mushrooms and garlic, salt and pepper, cayenne and basil. Turn mixture into a pie shell. Bake the quiche at 375F for 25 minutes or until it is golden. Serve hot.

Suggested Wine: Eggs are delicate, thus calling for a crisp, dry white wine. Cream cheese is also tangy. Consider Sauvignon Blanc, Pinot Grigio or Pinot Gris.

Brie and Maple-Cured Bacon Frittata
Serves 4

8 eggs
5 slices maple-cured bacon, cut into 1-inch pieces

½ (4.5-inch/8 oz./227 g) wheel of homemade Brie or Camembert, rind removed diced*

½-cup sliced mushrooms
1 tbsp. finely chopped fresh rosemary
3 tbsp. butter
2 cloves garlic, minced

*Use a cheese plane or vegetable peeler to remove rind of cheese. This recipe calls for a very ripened homemade Brie (soft and creamy.)

In a large bowl beat together eggs, bacon, cheese, mushrooms and rosemary. In a large skillet over medium heat, melt butter. Sauté garlic until soft. Increase heat to high. When butter begins to bubble, add egg mixture, shaking skillet to distribute ingredients evenly. Reduce heat to low and cook for 6 to 7 minutes. Using spatula, loosen egg mixture from sides of skillet and gradually from bottom. When frittata can slip in pan, invert a serving plate over the skillet. Flip the skillet, letting frittata fall onto the plate. Slide frittata back into pan and cook the other side until eggs are set, about 3 minutes. Serve hot.

Suggested Wine: Eggs are delicate and so require a crisp, dry white wine to match. Consider Sauvignon Blanc, Pinot Grigio or Pinot Gris.

Brie & Walnut Quesadillas with Cranberry Onion Relish
Serves 4-6
(makes 12 slices)

Cranberry onion relish:
2 tbsp. corn oil
1 small onion, thinly sliced
2 tsp. finely chopped fresh thyme
kosher salt to taste
freshly ground black pepper to taste
½-cup dried cranberries
½-cup dry white wine
1 tbsp. balsamic vinegar

Quesadillas:
4 tortillas (9 inches/23 cm in diameter)

1 (4.5-inch/8 oz./227 g) wheel of homemade Brie or Camembert, thinly sliced
¾-cup chopped walnuts, toasted*
corn oil (for frying)

*Walnuts can be toasted in a dry skillet over medium heat, tossing them frequently, for about 3 minutes.

To make the relish, heat 2 tbsp. oil in a skillet over low heat. Sauté the onion, thyme, salt and pepper for about 20 minutes, until the onion is almost caramelized. Add the cranberries, wine and vinegar. Simmer the mixture until no liquid remains. Remove it from the heat. Transfer it to a dish and let it cool.
To make the quesadillas, cover 2 tortillas with slices of cheese and sprinkle it with walnuts. Cover with another tortilla. Add 2 Tbsp (25 mL) of oil to the bottom of a large skillet. Heat the oil over medium heat. Fry the quesadillas until they're golden, about 1 to 2 minutes per side. Keep them warm. When you're ready to serve them, cut each into 6 slices. Serve them warm with a dipping bowl of Cranberry Onion Relish or place a dollop of the relish on each slice.

Suggested Wine: The cranberry relish has sweetness and so this dish requires an off-dry rose to match.

Camembert Fondue
Serves 4

1 clove garlic, halved
½-cup white wine
1/3-cup half and half cream

2 (4.5-inch/8 oz./227 g) wheels of homemade Camembert or Brie, rind removed, cubed*

1 tbsp. cornstarch
¼-cup brandy
1 loaf French baguette, cubed (for dunking)
4 apples, peeled and cubed (for dunking)

*Use a cheese plane or vegetable peeler to remove rind of cheese.

Rub the inside of a fondue pot with garlic. Pour in wine and cream. Heat over spirit lamp until bubbly. Over a low flame, add cheese, stirring constantly until cheese is completely melted. In a bowl whisk cornstarch into brandy. Add to cheese mixture, stirring for another 2 to 3 minutes. Serve fondue with cubed bread and cubed apple slices.

Suggested Wine: Because the apple slices are sweet, this fondue requires a white wine with some sweetness, such as an off-dry Riesling or off-dry Gewurztraminer.

Beef and Brie Wellington
With Madeira Sauce
Serves 4

4 (1 ½-inch-thick center-cut filets mignons, about 6 oz. each)
kosher salt to taste
freshly ground black pepper to taste
1 tbsp. unsalted butter
4 large mushrooms, thinly sliced
1 tbsp. finely chopped shallot
1 tbsp. minced garlic
1 large egg, lightly beaten for egg wash.
1 puff pastry sheet (from a 17 1/4-oz. package frozen puff pastry), thawed
½ (4.5-inch/8 oz./227 g) wheel of homemade Brie or Camembert, cut into 4 cubes

Sauce:
1-cup beef demi-glace
2 tbsp. Madeira

Preheat oven to 425F. Pat filets mignons dry with paper towel. Season with salt and pepper. In a shallow roasting pan roast filets in the middle of the oven for 12 minutes, or until the meat thermometer registers 110F (for rare). Let filets cool. Cover and refrigerate for at least 1 hour.

In a cast iron skillet, heat butter. Add mushroom slices, shallot and garlic. Cook over moderate heat, stirring, until mushrooms are lightly browned. Transfer mushroom mixture to a bowl to cool. In a small bowl beat an egg to make an egg wash.

On a lightly floured surface, roll out puff pastry sheet into a 14-inch square. Trim the edges to form a 13-inch square and cut the square into four 6 ½-inch squares.
Put 1 cube of cheese in center of 1 square and top it with one-fourth of the mushroom mixture. Top the mushroom mixture with a filet mignon, pressing it down gently, and wrap 2 opposite corners of puff pastry over the filet, overlapping them. Seal the seam with the egg wash. Wrap the remaining 2 corners of pastry over filet and seal it in the same manner. Seal any gaps with the egg wash and press pastry around filet to enclose it completely. Arrange beef Wellington, seam side down, on a baking sheet sprayed with non-stick cooking spray. Repeat the process 3 more times. Cover Wellingtons with plastic wrap and refrigerate for at least 2 hours or up to 1 day. (Chill remaining egg wash for brushing on pastry just before baking.)

Preheat oven to 425F. Brush the top and sides of each beef Wellington with some of the remaining egg wash and bake for 20 minutes, or until pastry is golden.

Suggested Wine: The richness and fattiness of this Wellington requires a red with forward fruit character. Consider Zinfandel, Shiraz or Merlot.

Brie and Parmigiano-Reggiano Tart
Serves 4 to 6

1 (17.3-oz.) package frozen puff pastry (2 sheets), thawed

Filling:
2 tbsp. butter

4 cups of leeks (white and green parts)
¼-cup water
kosher salt to taste

Custard:
2/3-cup whipping cream

1 (4.5-inch/8 oz./227 g) wheel of homemade Brie or Camembert, rind removed, cut into 1/2-inch pieces*

1 large egg
pinch of cayenne pepper
pinch of ground nutmeg
¼-cup freshly grated Parmigiano-Reggiano

*Use a cheese plane or vegetable peeler to remove rind of cheese.

Preheat the oven to 400F. Roll out each pastry sheet on a lightly floured surface to 12-inch square. Stack the sheets and roll out again to 15-inch square. Using a 14-inch pizza pan as a guide, cut the dough into a 14-inch round. (Like a pizza crust). Crimp the edges of the dough to form a ¼-inch rim. Transfer the dough to a baking sheet lined with parchment paper. Freeze 10 minutes.

In a cast iron skillet over medium heat, melt butter. Add leeks and water. Cook the leeks until tender, about 15 minutes. Season the leeks with salt. Transfer to a bowl. Set aside to cool.

Meanwhile to make the custard, in the same skillet bring the cream to a simmer. Reduce the heat to low. Add the Brie and stir until melted. Remove the skillet from the heat and cool for 5 minutes. Whisk in the egg, cayenne, and nutmeg. Set the custard aside.

Sprinkle Parmigiano over crust. Spread the leeks over. Drizzle custard over the leeks. Bake until the bottom is golden, about 20 minutes. Transfer to a rack to cool for 10 minutes. Serve warm or at room temperature.

Suggested Wine: The fattiness of the cheeses demands a big, fat white wine like barrel fermented and/or aged Chardonnay with at least 14% alcohol.

Chapter 6: Pasta, Polenta, Risotto

Spinach, Ricotta and Brie Lasagna
Serves 4

2 tbsp. olive oil
1 small onion, chopped
16 cremini mushrooms, chopped
2 cloves garlic minced
10 oz. fresh spinach, cooked and squeezed dry
kosher salt to taste
freshly ground black pepper to taste
1/4 tsp. nutmeg
2-cups homemade ricotta
1-cup chicken stock

3/4-cup half and half cream
1 (4.5-inch/8 oz./227 g) wheel of homemade Brie or Camembert, rind removed*
kosher salt to taste
freshly ground black pepper to taste
8 lasagna noodles, blanched in salt water
tomato sauce (as needed)
1 ½-cups grated mozzarella
fresh basil

*Use a cheese plane or vegetable peeler to remove rind of cheese.

In a cast iron skillet, add olive oil and sauté onions and mushrooms until soft. Add garlic and cook 3 minutes more. Add the spinach and heat through. Season the mixture with salt and pepper. Remove from heat and add the nutmeg. Stir in the ricotta. Transfer the ricotta mixture to a plate. Clean skillet.

In a cast iron skillet, heat chicken stock. Add cream and heat to a simmer. Add the cheese, a little at a time, and stir constantly. Bring to a boil and allow it to thicken for a minute. Remove from heat. Season the stock with salt and pepper.

To assemble, spray a lasagna dish with non-stick cooking spray. Spread layer of tomato sauce over sides and bottom of dish. Lay lasagna noodles on sauce, over lapping slightly. Add a layer of ricotta mixture. Add a layer of cheese sauce. Add a layer of grated mozzarella. Add lasagna noodles over grated mozzarella. Add layer of ricotta mixture. Add a layer of cheese sauce. Add a thick layer of grated mozzarella. Bake in a 350F oven for 30 minutes to heat thorough and then broil until the cheese bubbles. Serve hot, garnished with fresh basil.

Suggested Wine: The fattiness of this dish demands a barrel fermented and/or aged Chardonnay with at least 14% alcohol.

Crusted Mac and 3 Cheeses
Serves 4 to 6

4 single serving casserole dishes

1 ½-cups coarsely grated Gruyère cheese
1 ½-cups coarsely grated sharp Cheddar cheese (about 6 ounces)

¼-cup butter, divided
¼-cup all purpose flour
2 tsp. chopped fresh thyme leaves
3/4 tsp. nutmeg
4-cups whole milk

1 (4.5-inch/8 oz./227 g) wheels of homemade Brie or Camembert, rind removed and diced*

1 tbsp. butter
1 ¾-cups panko breadcrumbs
1 lb. macaroni pasta
8 tsp. whipping cream

*Use a cheese plane or vegetable peeler to remove rind of cheese.

Mix Gruyere and Cheddar. Set aside 1-cup of mixed cheeses for topping; cover remaining cheeses and chill. Melt butter in a large saucepan over medium heat. Add flour and stir until mixture turns golden brown, about 4 minutes. Add thyme and nutmeg. Gradually whisk in milk. Simmer until thickened and smooth, stirring often, about 4 minutes. Add Brie. Stir until melted and smooth.

Melt 1 tbsp. of butter in a cast iron skillet over medium-high heat. Add the breadcrumbs; toss. Stir until golden, about 2 minutes. Transfer breadcrumbs to a plate.

Preheat oven to 375F. In a large pot of boiling salted water cook pasta until tender, but still slightly hard. Drain. Transfer pasta to a large bowl. Pour Brie sauce over the pasta; toss. Divide the Mac and Cheese between individual casserole dishes. Sprinkle each dish with a 1/4-cup of the 1-cup of mixed Gruyere and Cheddar that you set aside. Place the casserole dishes on a baking sheet.

Sprinkle each dish with breadcrumbs. Bake pasta until beginning to bubble and the breadcrumbs are golden, about 20 minutes. Serve hot.

Suggested Wine: The fattiness from the cheese demands a big, fat white wine to match, such as a barrel fermented and/or aged Chardonnay with at least 14% alcohol.

Polenta with Camembert and Parmigiano-Reggiano
Serves 4

5 ½-cups (or more) chicken broth
1 garlic clove, pressed
1 ½-cups coarse-ground or regular white or yellow cornmeal

¾ (4.5-inch/8 oz./227 g) wheel of homemade Camembert or Brie, rind removed, cut into 1/2-inch pieces*

1 ¼-cups freshly grated Parmigiano-Reggiano
pinch cayenne pepper
kosher salt to taste
freshly ground black pepper to taste
pinch ground nutmeg

*Use a cheese plane or vegetable peeler to remove rind of cheese.

In a large saucepan bring 5 ½-cups chicken broth and garlic to a boil. Gradually add cornmeal, whisking until smooth. Reduce the heat to medium and simmer until thick and creamy, whisking constantly, about 8 minutes. Stir in Camembert and half of Parmigiano cheese. Season to taste with cayenne pepper, salt, pepper, and nutmeg. Whisk until polenta thickens slightly, about 2 minutes. Transfer to a large bowl. Sprinkle with remaining Parmigiano cheese and serve on the table, hot.

Suggested Wine: The fattiness of this polenta demands a big, fat white wine, such as barrel fermented and/or aged Chardonnay with at least 14% alcohol.

Risotto with Cauliflower, Camembert and Almonds
Serves 4

6-cups chicken broth
3 thyme sprigs, plus 1 tsp. leaves
1 tbsp. butter
2 tbsp. olive oil, divided
4-cups of cauliflower florets
1 ½-cups Arborio rice
1/3-cup dry white wine

½ (4.5-inch/8 oz./227 g) wheel of homemade Camembert or Brie rind removed, diced

1/3-cup sliced almonds, toasted*
kosher salt to taste
freshly ground black pepper to taste

*Toast almonds in a dry fry pan until golden.

In a saucepan over medium heat, bring broth and thyme sprigs to a simmer.

In a cast iron skillet heat butter and oil over medium-high heat. Sauté the cauliflower until crisp-tender and golden brown, about 6 minutes. Add the thyme leaves and sauté for another minute. Transfer to a bowl.

Using the same skillet (as used for cauliflower) add remaining tbsp. of oil, then add rice and cook, stirring constantly for about 1 minute. Add wine and simmer, stirring, until wine has been absorbed, about 1 minute. Add ½-cup hot broth and simmer, stirring, until broth has been absorbed. Continue simmering and adding more hot broth as needed, about ½-cup at a time, stirring constantly and waiting until each addition has been absorbed before adding the next one, until the rice is just tender and looks creamy, 18 to 22 minutes. (There will be leftover broth.)

Fold the cauliflower and Camembert into the risotto, and season to taste with salt and pepper. Thin the risotto if needed with some of remaining hot broth. Divide between plates and garnish each one with toasted almonds.

Suggested Wine: The cheese and creaminess of the risotto calls for a big, fat white wine, such as a barrel fermented and/or aged Chardonnay with at least 14% alcohol.

Bacon Mac and Brie
Serves 4 to 6

4 oz. sliced bacon, cut into 1-inch strips
1 medium onion, thinly sliced

1 tbsp. all-purpose flour
1-cup whole milk

2 (4.5-inch/8 oz./227 g) wheel of homemade Camembert or Brie, rind removed, cut into 1-inch chunks*

1 lb. macaroni
kosher salt to taste
freshly ground black pepper to taste
¼-cup of freshly grated Parmigiano-Reggiano cheese
1-cup of panko crumbs

*Use a cheese plane or vegetable peeler to remove rind of cheese.

Preheat the broiler. In a cast iron skillet, fry the bacon until crispy, about 6 minutes. Drain on paper towels. Leave ¼ of bacon fat in the skillet. Add the onion and cook, softening, about 1 minute. Set onion on a plate. Add flour to the skillet and cook until browned. Add the milk and stir, removing any lumps, making a roux sauce. Heat the milk until steaming. Slowly add the cheese, a few chunks at a time until melted, stirring constantly.

Meanwhile, in a large pot of boiling salted water, cook the macaroni leaving it slightly hard; drain. Add the fusilli to the cheese sauce and toss. Add the bacon and season the pasta with salt and pepper. Transfer the pasta to an 8-inch baking dish sprayed with non-stick cooking spray. In a bowl combine Parmigiano-Reggiano and panko crumbs. Sprinkle the panko mixture on top of the pasta casserole. Broil until the crust is golden, about 3 to 5 minutes. Watch carefully so the breadcrumbs do not burn. Serve hot.

Suggested Wine: The fattiness of the cream sauce on this pasta needs a big, fat white wine, such as barrel fermented and/or aged Chardonnay with at least 14% alcohol.

Fettuccine with Double Smoked Bacon, Brie and Rosemary
Serves 4

3 cloves garlic, minced

1/2 lb. double smoked bacon, chopped
½-cup half and half cream
½-cup chicken broth
1-cup freshly grated Parmigiano-Reggiano
freshly ground black pepper to taste

½ (4.5-inch/8 oz./227 g) wheel homemade Camembert or Brie, rind removed, thinly sliced*

1 lb. fettuccine
rosemary sprigs (for garnish)

*Use a cheese plane or vegetable peeler to remove rind of cheese.

In a cast iron skillet over medium heat cook garlic until soft. Cook bacon pieces until golden, about 6 minutes. Transfer bacon to a plate lined with paper towel to drain. Discard fat from skillet. To same skillet add half and half cream and chicken broth and bring to boil over medium heat. Reduce heat to low. Add Parmigiano and stir until cheese melts. Season to taste with pepper. Add Brie, stirring constantly until cheese melts.

Meanwhile, in a large pot of boiling salted water cook pasta until al dente. Drain. Transfer noodles to the skillet. Toss with the sauce. Divide the pasta between bowels. Garnish each bowl with a sprig of fresh rosemary. Serve hot.

Suggested Wine: The fattiness of the cream sauce on this pasta needs a big, fat white wine, such as barrel fermented and/or aged Chardonnay with at least 14% alcohol.

Chapter 7: Entrees

Baked Chicken with Camembert and White Wine And Brie
Serves 4

1-cup white wine
4 skinless, boneless chicken breasts
kosher salt to taste
freshly ground black pepper to taste
1 (4.5-inch/8 oz./227 g) wheel of homemade Camembert or Brie, sliced

Preheat oven to 400F. Pour the wine into a baking dish large enough to hold 4 breasts. Season the breasts with salt and pepper. Bake until the juices run clear, about 35minutes. When chicken is done, slice 3 cavities in the breasts, about 3-inches long. Be sure not to slice through to bottom. Place slices of cheese in the cavities. Place baking dish back into the oven and bake until cheese slices have melted. Serve hot with fresh salads of green.

Suggested Wine: Choose a big, fat white with enough fattiness to match the creaminess of the melted Brie. A barrel fermented and aged Chardonnay with at least 14% alcohol is ideal.

Guinea Fowl with Brie and Hazelnuts

Serves 4

Filling:
1 medium pear, peeled
1 slice white bread, crust removed, diced

½ (4.5-inch/8 oz./227 g) wheel of homemade Brie or Camembert, rind removed, diced*

3 tbsp. chopped hazelnuts
Pinch pepper

4 boneless, skinless guinea fowl breasts (or chicken breasts), ¼ lb. each
3 tbsp. melted butter
16 sheets phyllo pastry (6-inches x 4-inches)

Sauce:
1 medium shallot, sliced
½ clove garlic, sliced
1-cup white wine
1-cup whipping cream
½ (4.5-inch/8 oz./227 g) wheel of homemade Brie or Camembert, diced*
kosher salt to taste
freshly ground black pepper to taste

*Use a cheese plane or vegetable peeler to remove rind of cheese.

In a pot of boiling water poach pear until tender-crisp. Drain. Core and dice. To make the filling, in a bowl mix pear, bread, cheese, hazelnuts and pepper. In each guinea fowl breast, cut a pocket 2-inches long and ¼-inch deep. Stuff each pocket with ¼ of the filling.

On a work surface, lay out a phyllo sheet. Brush with melted butter. Top with another sheet. Brush with butter. Continue until 4 sheets have been used. Place a stuffed breast at one end of the phyllo. Fold in the sides. Roll the breast until wrapped in pastry. Repeat procedure until all the breasts are wrapped in pastry. Place wrapped breasts, seam side down, on a baking sheet lined with parchment paper. Brush phyllo pouches lightly with butter. Bake at 325F for 15 to 20 minutes or until the phyllo is golden and crispy. Set aside.

To make the sauce, in a cast iron skillet over medium heat, combine shallot, garlic and wine. Reduce to one quarter in volume. Stir in the cream. Reduce by half. Stirring constantly and slowly, add the diced cheese. Season with salt and pepper. Keep warm. Spoon sauce onto each warmed plate. Set wrapped breast on sauce. Slice breast into 4 slices.

Suggested Wine: The fattiness of the butter in the phyllo and cheese demands a big, fat white to match, such as a barrel fermented and/or aged Chardonnay with at least 14% alcohol.

Lamb Loins with Spinach, Cognac and Brie
Serves 4

2 lamb loins (2 lb. each with bones)
bones and trimmings reserved*

Stock:
2/3-cup mirepoix (diced carrots, onion, celery, leeks)
1 tsp. tomato paste
¼-cup cognac
2-cups water
pinch kosher salt

Stuffing:
1-cup fresh spinach
1/2 (4.5-inch/8 oz./227 g) wheel of homemade Brie or Camembert

kosher salt to taste
freshly ground black pepper to taste
1 tbsp. finely chopped fresh rosemary

Sauce:
1 tbsp. vegetable oil
2 shallots, chopped
¼-cup white wine
¼-cup whipping cream
½ (4.5-inch/8 oz./227 g) wheel of homemade Brie or Camembert, diced

*Have your butcher bone and trim the lamb.

Set trimmings aside. To make the stock, in a roasting pan roast lamb bones at 450F until burned, about 1.5 hours. Add mirepoix. Cook for another 20 to 30 minutes. Transfer bones and mirepoix to a large saucepan. Stir in the tomato paste. Set roasting pan over high heat. Deglaze with cognac, scraping up brown bits. Pour liquid over the bones. Bring the liquid to a boil. Reduce the heat and simmer, covered, for 2 hours. Season stock to taste with salt. Set aside.

To make the stuffing, blanch spinach. Drain and cool. In a food processor or blender, combine spinach, lamb trimmings, cheese, salt, pepper and rosemary. Process until smooth.

Fill a piping bag with stuffing. Using a wooden spoon to hold open the incision, pipe stuffing into the cavities. Tie loins with kitchen string to keep the stuffing in place. Rub olive oil lightly over the loins. In a cast iron skillet over medium heat, brown loins on all sides, about 90 seconds each side. Arrange loins in the roasting pan sprayed with non-stick cooking spray. Roast at 375F for 5 minutes for rare, 15 minutes for well done. Keep warm.

Meanwhile make the sauce. In the same skillet over medium heat, heat the oil. Sauté the shallots until soft. Increase the heat to medium-high and add the wine. Reduce the heat. Simmer, reducing by half. Stir in the cream. Reduce by 1/4. Add the cheese, stirring constantly until the cheese melts. Remove the string from the loins. Slice the loins into medallions. Arrange medallions on serving plates. Spoon the sauce around the lamb loins.

Suggested Wine: The fattiness of lamb and Brie calls for an austere red wine to match. Consider Malbec, Cabernet Sauvignon or Cabernet Franc.

Roasted Beef Rouladen in Sweet Pepper Crust with Camembert Sauce
Serves 4

Medallions:
2 tsp. vegetable oil
4 medallions of beef (2 oz. each)
kosher salt to taste
freshly ground black pepper to taste

Rouladen:
2 tsp. vegetable oil
¼-cup thin onion rings
4 slices beef
1 tbsp. Dijon mustard
1 2/3-cup brown stock

Beef in Sweet Pepper Crust:
¼-cup mixed diced sweet green, yellow and red peppers
2 tbsp. dried breadcrumbs
2 tbsp. egg whites
½ lb. beef strip loin
kosher salt to taste
freshly ground black pepper to taste

Roasted Garlic and Brie Sauce:
1 tsp. olive oil
1 tbsp. minced garlic
¼-cup chicken stock

½ (4.5-inch/8 oz./227 g) wheel of homemade Camembert or Brie, rind removed, cubed*

kosher salt to taste
freshly ground black pepper to taste

Season medallions with salt and pepper. In a cast iron skillet over medium heat, heat oil. Sauté the medallions for 3 minutes on each side. Keep warm. Season with salt and pepper.

*Use a cheese plane or vegetable peeler to remove rind of cheese.

To make the roulade, in the same skillet over medium heat, heat the oil. Sweat the onions for 3 minutes. Brush meat slices with mustard. Top meat slices with onion. Roll up slices, securing each with kitchen string or a toothpick. In the same skillet over medium heat, reheat the oil. Sear roulade until golden on all sides, about 1 minute. Add brown stock. Bring to a boil. Transfer the cast iron skillet to a 350F oven and braise meat for 40 minutes. Transfer the roulade to a plate. Remove the string. Keep warm. In the same skillet over medium-high heat, reduce the stock to 1-cup. Transfer to a container. Keep warm. Clean the skillet.

To make sweet pepper crust, in a small bowl stir together peppers, breadcrumbs and egg whites. Season the strip loin with salt and pepper. Place the strip-loins in a 13 by 9-inch baking dish. Roast at 350F for 2 minutes for rare, longer for medium rare. Divide the crust into 4. Place ¼ of the crust over each strip-loin. Bake another 8 minutes or until the crust is golden. Let the strip-loins rest for 5 minutes. Keep warm.

To make the sauce, in the cleaned skillet over medium heat, heat the oil. Sauté the garlic until golden. Dry garlic on paper towel. In a blender or food processor blend the garlic with the chicken stock. With motor running, slowly add the Camembert, blending until smooth. Season the sauce with salt and pepper. Spoon ¼-cup of the reduced stock onto each plate. Pour 4 tsp. of sauce into the stock. Swirl with a wooden skewer. Arrange medallions, roulade and strip-loin crusted beef on the sauce. Serve hot.

Suggested Wine: Choose an austere red wine with enough flavour and fattiness to stand up to this rich beef dish. Consider Cabernet Sauvignon, Cabernet Franc or Malbec.

Beef and Veal Tenderloin with Mousse of Crab and Camembert Cheese Wrapped in a Romano Cheese Crepe
Serves 4

2/3 lb. beef tenderloin ends
2/3 lb. veal tenderloin ends

Mousse:
6 crab legs, meat only (reserve shells for sauce)
½ (4.5-inch/8 oz./227 g) wheel of homemade Camembert or Brie, cubed
1/3-cup whipping cream
1 egg white
kosher salt to taste
freshly ground black pepper to taste

Crepes:
½-cup all-purpose flour
1-cup milk
2 eggs
½-cup grated Romano cheese
2 tbsp. butter, melted
kosher salt to taste
freshly ground black pepper to taste
3 tbsp. butter, melted

Sauce:
Leftover crab shells
4 tsp. olive oil
2/3-cup mirepoix (diced carrots, onion, celery, leek)
2 tbsp. tomato paste
½-cup white wine
1-cup demi-glace*
¼-cup cognac
¼-cup unsalted butter, softened and cubed

kosher salt to taste
freshly ground black pepper to taste
dash hot sauce

4 cooked crab claws (for garnish)

From the beef tenderloin ends cut 6 fillets about 4-inches long and 2 oz. in weight. From the veal tenderloin ends cut 6 fillets about 4-inches long and 2 oz. in weight. Set aside.

To make the mousse, cut remaining meat into small chunks. In a food processor or blender grind the meat. Add the Camembert and blend well. With the motor running, slowly add the cream. Add the egg white. Pour the mixture into a bowl. Fold in the crabmeat from the leg shells. Season the mixture with salt and pepper. Put the bowl over the ice and refrigerate until needed.

To make crepe batter, put flour in a large bowl. Push flour to one side. In a small bowl beat eggs with milk. Pour the milk beside the flour. Gradually whisk the flour into the milk until the batter is smooth. Stir in the Romano cheese and 2 tbsp. of melted butter. Season the batter with salt and pepper. Cover and refrigerate for 1 hour.

Meanwhile, make the sauce. In a case iron skillet over medium heat, combine the crab leg shells and oil. Transfer the skillet to the oven. Roast the shells at 350F for 15 minutes. Remove the skillet from the oven. Add the mirepoix and tomato paste. Place the skillet back into the oven and continue roasting until the paste turns brown but the carrots are golden, about 15 minutes. Remove the skillet from the oven and add the white wine and demi glace. Place on the stove and over low heat and simmer for 30 minutes, until the mixture is reduced to 1/3. Add the cognac. Simmer for 2 more minutes. Keep warm.

Meanwhile make 4 crepes. Brush a 6-inch non-stick crepe pan with 2 tsp. melted butter. Set the pan over medium heat. Spoon in 2 tbsp. batter. Swirl the pan until the batter covers the bottom. Cook until the surface looks dry, about 30 seconds. Set the crepes on a plate and cover with a towel to keep from drying out while making 5 more crepes. On a work surface lay out the crepes. Spread mousse down the centre of each crepe. Lay a beef and veal fillet side by side over the mouse. Spread remaining mousse over the fillets. Fold 2 sides tightly over the filling. Brush the tops of the crepes with 3 tbsp. melted butter. Lay the crepes on a baking sheet. Bake the crepes at 350F for 10 to 15 minutes or until the mousse is cooked through.

Meanwhile, whisk the butter into the sauce, one cube at a time. Season the sauce with salt, pepper and hot sauce. Spoon the sauce onto each plate. When crepes have cooled slightly, slice in 3 lengthwise, and arrange on the sauce. Garnish each plate with a cooked crab claw.

Suggested Wine: The richness and complexity of flavors in this dish requires an austere red wine to match. Consider Cabernet Sauvignon, Cabernet Franc or Malbec.

Turkey, Camembert and Prosciutto Roulades
Serves 4

3 (2 lb.) turkey breasts, boneless

Stuffing:
3 Poblano chilies

1 (4.5-inch/8 oz./227 g) wheel of homemade Camembert or Brie, rind removed, diced*

1 ½-cups freshly grated Gruyere cheese

Cordon Bleu:
honey mustard (as needed)
15 slices prosciutto
kosher salt as needed
freshly ground black pepper as needed
vegetable oil (as needed)

*Use a cheese plane or vegetable peeler to remove rind of cheese.

Preheat broiler. To pound turkey breast, chill breast for 30 minutes before starting. Chilling will make the meat easier to handle and will help the meat maintain its firmness. Place a breast into a plastic resealable freezer bag. Place the bag on a cutting board. Pound the breast to ¼-inch thickness. Repeat process for all 3 breasts.

Broil Poblano chilies until charred and blistered, turning as needed. Transfer chilies to bowl and cover with plastic wrap to sweat them. Let stand for 10 minutes. Peel chilies, remove the skins and seeds. Finely chop the chilies and add them to the cheeses. Combine the cheeses and chilies together to make stuffing. Set aside.

Preheat oven to 375F. Coat each turkey cutlet with honey mustard. Lay 5 slices of prosciutto on each cutlet, trimming to leave a small boarder around the edge. Divide the stuffing into thirds. Spread the stuffing onto each cutlet, leaving a small boarder around the edge. Starting from one side, tightly roll up cutlet away from you, making sure the stuffing doesn't escape. Secure the roll (called a roulade) with butcher's twine every 2 inches to form a tight, long log. Repeat the process for all 3 breasts. Season the roulades with salt and pepper.

In a cast iron skillet, heat oil and brown the roulades on all sides. Transfer the cast iron skillet (with roulades) to the oven and roast for about 20 to 30 minutes or until meat is done (reaching 160F). To serve, remove the twine from roulades and slice them into ½-inch slices. Divide between 4 plates. Drizzle with pan juices.

Suggested Wine: While gentle, the honey mustard gives the roulades a slight sweetness requiring a white wine with sweetness, such as an off-dry Riesling or off-dry Gewürztraminer.

Lobster and Brie Casserole
Serves 4 to 6

Casserole:

Kosher salt
1 lb. dried egg noodles
2 tbsp. unsalted butter
2 shallots, minced
3 cloves garlic, minced
3 tbsp. fresh oregano
1 cup dry white wine
1 cup fish stock

1 (4.5-inch/8 oz./227 g) wheel of homemade Brie or Camembert, rind removed, diced*

2 cups crabmeat

Topping:
1 pkg. dried shiitake mushrooms
½-cup panko breadcrumbs
2 tbsp. butter

*Use a cheese plane or vegetable peeler to remove rind of cheese.

In a large pot of boiling, salted water cook egg noodles until just tender, but not soft. Drain and set aside.

Preheat oven to 350F. In a cast iron skillet over medium heat, melt butter and sauté shallots until tender, about 4 minutes. Add garlic and oregano. Cook another 2 minutes. Add wine and let simmer until the wine is reduced by half. Add stock. Fold in Brie. Remove skillet from heat. Fold in egg noodles. Fold in lobster. Transfer to a casserole-baking dish.

In a food processor or blender, grind mushrooms. In a bowl combine ground mushrooms and panko breadcrumbs. In a cast iron skillet melt butter. Add breadcrumbs and mix to coat breadcrumbs with butter. Sprinkle breadcrumbs over casserole. Bake until heated through and breadcrumbs are golden, about 7 to 10 minutes. Serve hot.

Suggested Wine: The richness from the cheese and lobster demands a big, fat white wine, such as a barrel fermented and aged Chardonnay with at least 14% alcohol.

Grilled Pork Chops with Camembert and Cashews
Serves 4

4 (1 ¼ lb.) boneless pork loin chops
kosher salt to taste
freshly ground black pepper to taste
2 tbsp. olive oil
1/4 cup marmalade, melted
4 rounds (1/4-inch) cored and peeled fresh pineapple
½ (4.5-inch/8 oz./227 g) wheel of homemade Brie or Camembert, sliced
¼-cup salted roasted cashews*

*Cashews can be roasted in dry fry pan.

Preheat oven to 350F. Sprinkle chops with salt and pepper. In a cast iron skillet over medium heat, heat oil. Panfry chops for about 4 minutes. Turn the chops and spread the other side with a thick coat of marmalade. Add a slice of pineapple to each chop. Cover the skillet with foil. Transfer skillet to oven. Roast chops until juices run clean in skillet, about 22 to 25 minutes. Make sure the chops are not over cooked. Remove the foil. Add a slice of Brie to the top of pineapple slice on each chop. Turn on the broiler. Broil until the cheese has melted. Transfer to plates and garnish with cashews. Serve hot.

Suggested Wine: The sweetness from the pineapple calls for a white wine with plenty of sweetness, such as a late harvest Riesling or late harvest Gewurztraminer.

Chapter 8: Desserts

Pastry Wrapped Brie with Cranberry Orange Sauce
Serves 4 to 6

Cranberry Sauce:
1 (12-oz.) bag of fresh cranberries
1-cup sugar
1-cup fresh orange juice
1 tsp. grated orange peel
1 medium seedless orange (peel and pith removed), fruit diced
¾-cup walnuts, toasted, cut into 1/2-inch pieces*

All-purpose flour, for dusting
1 standard package frozen puff pastry, thawed
1 (4.5-inch/8 oz./227 g) wheel of homemade Brie or Camembert
1 small egg yolk
1 tbsp. heavy cream
½-cup cranberry sauce
fresh mint for garnish

*Walnuts can be toasted in dry fry pan, tossed over medium heat

To make cranberry sauce, combine the first 4 ingredients in medium saucepan; bring to a boil, stirring until sugar dissolves. Lower the heat. Cook until the cranberries are tender and mixture thickens, stirring occasionally, about 12 minutes. Remove the sauce from the heat. Let it cool. Fold in diced orange and walnuts. Transfer to a bowl. Cover and refrigerator for at least 6 hours and up to 3 days.

Line a baking sheet with parchment paper. Set aside. Dust work surface with flour. Place a sheet of puff pastry on the work surface. Roll out the puff pastry until it is very thin, slightly less than 1/8-inch thick. Using a sharp knife and a pizza pan as a guide, cut the puff pastry into a 13-inch round, reserving scraps. Place the Brie in the center of the puff pastry. Fold puff pastry up and over Brie to enclose. Transfer the pastry to a baking sheet sprayed with non-stick cooking spray.

In a small bowl, combine egg yolk and cream to make an egg wash. Using a pastry brush, gently brush pastry with the egg wash. Transfer to refrigerator and chill for at least 30 minutes and up to overnight.

Preheat oven to 400F degrees. Bake Brie until golden brown and puffed, about 40 minutes. Remove Brie from the oven. Transfer to a serving plate. Cover Brie with ½-cup of the cranberry sauce. Garnish with fresh mint.

Suggested Wine: The sweetness of this dish calls for a wine with mega sweetness such as a Cabernet Franc Icewine.

Baked Ripened Camembert with Mango
Serves 4

1 (4.5-inch/8 oz./227 g) wheel of homemade Camembert or Brie, with rind
2 tbsp. apricot or peach preserve
2 mangoes, peeled and sliced thinly
crackers (as needed)

Preheat oven to 400F. Cut the Camembert in half horizontally. Spread preserve evenly over cheese. Lay slices of mango on top. Place top half of cheese on fruit. Wrap cheese wheel in foil. Place on a baking sheet and bake 15 minutes or until cheese is runny. Serve hot with dried fruit and nut crackers.

Suggested Wine: The sweetness in the mango requires a white wine with sweetness. Consider an off-dry Riesling or off-dry Gewürztraminer.

Camembert with Fresh Fig Compote and Blue Cheese
Serves 4

1 (4.5-inch/8 oz./227 g) wheel of homemade Camembert or Brie
1 large egg, beaten to blend
1-cup fresh breadcrumbs
1-cup ruby Port
1-cup fresh figs, halved lengthwise
2 tbsp. honey
2 tbsp. butter
1/3-cup crumbled blue cheese

1 French bread baguette, sliced into rounds, lightly toasted

Brush Camembert on all sides with egg, then coat with breadcrumbs. Cover in plastic wrap and refrigerate for at least 1 hour.

In a cast iron skillet over medium heat bring Port to a boil. Add figs. Simmer until heated through, about 3 minutes. Using a slotted spoon, transfer figs to a small bowl. Add honey to Port in pan; boil until reduced to thick syrup, stirring occasionally, about 5 minutes. Pour syrup over figs.

In a cast iron skillet melt butter. Add coated Camembert and cook until breadcrumbs are golden and cheese is warmed inside. Transfer Camembert to a platter. Top with fig mixture. Sprinkle with crumbled blue cheese. Serve with dried fruit and nut crackers.

Suggested Wine: The sweetness in this cheese dessert requires a sweet Port, like Tawny Port, to match.

Apple and Camembert Baked Pastry
Serves 4 to 6

11 sheet frozen puff pastry (see note)
1 large egg
1 tbsp. water
1 large Granny Smith apple, peeled, cored, cut in half vertically
juice from ½ fresh lemon in ¼ cup water
2 tbsp. butter
½-cup firmly packed light brown sugar

1 (4.5-inch/8 oz./227 g) wheel of homemade Camembert or Brie, sliced in half horizontally

Thaw puff pastry sheet at room temperature for 30 minutes. Preheat oven to 400F. Combine egg and water in a small bowl. Set aside.

Cut apple into very thin slices. Transfer apple slices to bowl of lemon water. In a cast iron skillet over low heat add butter, brown sugar and apple slices. Sauté until apple slices are softened, about 5 minutes. Transfer to a bowl and let cool.

Unfold pastry sheet onto a lightly floured surface and roll into a

14-inch square. Cut off the corners to make a circle. Place one half of Camembert, cut side up, in center of pastry sheet. Top with half of apple mixture. Place remaining top of Camembert, cut side down, on top of apples. Top with remaining apple mixture. Brush edges of pastry with egg mixture and fold pastry over the cheese. Press edges to seal. Place the cheese pastry, seam side down, on a baking sheet sprayed with non-stick cooking spray. Brush the top of the pastry with the remaining egg mixture.

Bake until golden brown, about 20 minutes. Let stand for 15 minutes before serving.

Suggested Wine: The sweetness from this dessert calls for a very sweet white wine, such as Riesling Icewine.

Printed in Poland
by Amazon Fulfillment
Poland Sp. z o.o., Wrocław